Flute of Milk, Susan Fealy's first full-scale book, is a quiet, deep-running volume. The poems play off art and the senses, the mind and the possibility of cultivating a soul. The poet enters art and life where 'Memory prefers to hold things still, / but the past, present and future / are a long flute of milk.' It's within the darkness that Wittgenstein placed two roses, one red one white, that Fealy questions the power of the imagination: 'But who, if not ourselves, are we? / Is a rose red in the dark?'

I read this book over three weeks, and with each consecutive reading the poems flowed together, revealing deeper bays and channels of lyrical richness. The poems are pared back and clean, like the images and verbal brush marks in the poem about Vermeer's painting *The Milkmaid*. The colour blue drifts through the volume, carrying 'the soft blood of roses', 'a force of herons or anxious angels', and a lover who offers nothing but 'the terror of his faith'. There are words that hang on black wings and poems that contain a world of bees, places where 'forget-me-nots break / across bone', a tenderness with an edge. There are poems that describe the process of turning bodies into song. This is a remarkable book, delicate, tough, sensual, spiked with ideas and lines that create the deep music of real poetry.

Robert Adamson

Other titles in the UWAP Poetry series (established 2016)

Our Lady of the Fence Post by J. H. Crone
Border Security by Bruce Dawe
Melbourne Journal by Alan Loney
Star Struck by David McCooey
Dark Convicts by Judy Johnson
Rallying by Quinn Eades
A Personal History of Vision by Luke Fischer
Charlie Twirl by Alan Gould
Snake Like Charms by Amanda Joy

Flute of Milk

Susan Fealy

Susan Fealy is a Melbourne-based poet, writer and clinical psychologist. She began writing and publishing poetry in 2007 and was a managing co-editor at Five Islands Press (2009–2010). Her poems have been published widely in Australian journals, newspapers and anthologies including *Best Australian Poems 2009*, *2010* and *2013*. Others appear in internationally-sourced anthologies including *Villanelles* (Everyman's Library Pocket Poets, 2012). Among awards for her poetry are the NSW Society of Women Writers National Poetry Prize 2013 and the Henry Kendall Poetry Award 2010. Her work was selected for the May 2016 Australian Poets issue of *Poetry* (Chicago).

Susan Fealy
Flute of Milk

Poetry

First published in 2017 by
UWA Publishing
Crawley, Western Australia 6009
www.uwap.uwa.edu.au

UWAP is an imprint of UWA Publishing
a division of The University of Western Australia

This book is copyright. Apart from any fair dealing
for the purpose of private study, research, criticism
or review, as permitted under the *Copyright Act 1968*,
no part may be reproduced by any process without
written permission.
Enquiries should be made to the publisher.

Copyright © Susan Fealy 2017
The moral right of the author has been asserted.

National Library of Australia
Cataloguing-in-Publication entry:
Fealy, Susan, author.
Flute of milk / Susan Fealy.
ISBN: 9781742589398 (paperback)
Australian poetry—21st century.

Designed by Becky Chilcott, Chil3
Typeset in Lyon Text by Lasertype
Printed by Lightning Source

For my mother and father,
Beverley and Ivan Fealy,
and for my first poetry mentors,
Judith Rodriguez and Ron Pretty

Contents

Part One
Made in Delft **15**
Flute of Milk **16**
A Confluence of Blues **18**
In the Formal Wear Shop **20**
Intimidations **22**
In Lieu of a Statue **23**
Faith is Green **24**
What Memory is Like **26**
Black on the Tongue **28**
A Measure of Flying **29**
A Voice for Hands **30**
Lake Mungo **31**

How to Dive in Kelp Forest **32**
Apple Days **33**
Sculpting into Mind **34**
A Poem **35**

Part Two
Almost Palimpsest **39**
The Price of Honey **40**
Seeing the Pregnant Woman at Pompeii **41**
Discovered in 1977: *Petrogale persephone* **42**
Flight **43**
Bringing You Home **44**

Instructions for Weaning a Baby 45
A Mermaid's Story 46
Mycophobia 47
Breast Imaging 48
Frames for Better or Worse 50
We Outgrow Love like Other
Things 52
In the Cemetery 54
This World is not Conclusion 55
Metamorphosis 56
The Hope Stone 57
The Striped Moth 58
from Notes on Art and Dying 59
Film 60

Gouache, Sheep Skulls, Fence
Bracket 63
For Cornflowers to Sing 65
The Vase Imposes 66
Southern Ice Porcelain 68
The Wabi-sabi Storage Jar 69
Everest 70
The Danger of Lilies 71
Two Voices 72
Writing with the Left Hand 73

Notes 75

Acknowledgements

A number of these poems, some in earlier versions, have appeared in the following journals and anthologies: *Antipodes, Australian Book Review, Australian Poetry Journal, Axon, Cordite, Etchings, Eureka Street, Images, Island, Mascara Literary Review, Meanjin, Poetry* (Chicago), *Rabbit, Weekend Australian, Westerly, Australian Love Poems 2013* (Inkerman & Blunt, 2013), *Award Winning Australian Writing 2014* (Melbourne Books, 2014), *Contemporary Australian Feminist Poetry* (Hunter Publishers, 2016), *Off the Path* (Central Coast Poets Inc., 2010), *Prayers of a Secular World* (Inkerman & Blunt, 2015), *The Best Australian Poems 2009, 2010* and *2013* (Black Inc.), *The Green Fuse* (Picaro Press, 2010), *Villanelles* (Everyman's Library Pocket Poets, 2012); also in ezines *The Merri Creek: Poems and Pieces*, Collected Works—Poetry & Ideas Blogspot, *Tuesday Poem* (Australia); and websites *University of Tasmania, School of Philosophy*.

'The Price of Honey' was highly commended in the Eastern Libraries National Poetry Competition, 2009. 'Metamorphosis' won first prize in the Henry Kendall Poetry Award, 2010. 'How to Dive in Kelp Forest' was highly commended in the Inaugural Place and Experience Poetry Prize, 2010. 'A Voice for Hands' won second prize in the Tom Collins Poetry Prize, 2010. 'Flight' was awarded third prize in the NSW Society of Women Writers National Poetry Prize, 2011; 'In Lieu of a Statue' was highly commended in the same competition. 'The Hope Stone' won first prize in the NSW Society of Women Writers National Poetry Prize 2013. 'Gouache, Sheep Skulls, Fence Bracket' and 'Film' were highly commended in the Tom Collins Poetry Prize, 2013. Grateful acknowledgement is made to the publishers, editors and judges.

My profound gratitude to Debbie Lim, Alex Skovron, Mark Tredinnick, Michelle Cahill, Catherine McKeown, Jacinta Le Plastrier and Robert Adamson who read the manuscript and contributed valuable suggestions. Special thanks to Ron Pretty, Judith Rodriguez, Kris Hemensley, Claire Potter, Anne Elvey and Jennifer Compton for their critique of particular poems. Many thanks to my editor Terri-ann White and the team at UWAP for making this first book possible and for giving their warm support and expertise along the way.

Individual poems in this book are dedicated to:

'Faith is Green' for Peter Steele (1939–2012)
'A Poem' and 'Seeing the Pregnant Woman at Pompeii' for Debbie Lim
'Flight' for Ron Pretty
'Two Voices' and 'Instructions for Weaning a Baby' for Claire Potter
'Southern Ice Porcelain' for Les Blakebrough
'Everest' for Harley

I gave you all you needed:
bed of earth, blanket of blue air—
Louise Glück, 'Retreating Wind'

Made in Delft

after *The Milkmaid*
by Johannes Vermeer

White walls *melken* the daylight.
In this plain room
The map of the world
Has been painted over:
Only a woman, blond
Light from the window,
Her wide-mouthed jug
And bread on the table.
Vision slows at her wrist,
Travels along her forearm.
Her apron cascades
Lapis lazuli.
One can almost touch her thick
Waist, her generous shoulders,
Her crisp linen cap.
One can almost taste the milk
Escaping her jug.

Flute of Milk

after *The Sea*
by John Banville

Inside the dairy, washed so white
it approaches blue,
muslin-draped pans of milk
dream in their silence
and two steel milk-churns
(sentries in flat hats)
burn with white rosettes:
light held from the sun.
I remember the butter churn—
the handle I never turned.
Memory prefers to hold things still,
but the past, present and future
are a long flute of milk.
I am washing my hands: a spot
on the curve of the hand-basin
streams out like a nebula.
I remember washing her hair—
pouring water from a jug.
The sluice fell on the crown of her head.
Beads broke in a silver string,
like the bracelet around her wrist,
that diadem of our night swim.
The water flowed and flowed over our arms,
undulations of black satin.

She stands unshadowed now
in milky light—her face
seems almost featureless
as if the profile of a coin.
Be anyone you like, she said.
But who, if not ourselves, are we?
Is a rose red in the dark?
I wash some colour here, scumble
a detail there. Her portrait
will never be done.

A Confluence of Blues

A certain blue penetrates your soul.
—Henri Matisse

Isatis tinctoria,
those lemon-yellow flowers,
flakes of snow that didn't melt—
somehow absorbed the sun.

Soak its reluctant leaves
in human urine,
immerse the fabric for a day,
peg it out in the sun.

Watch as it converts to blue.

Ai-gami, a fading blue
from the day flower, *Commelina.*

Indigo, a lasting blue
from leaves stitched to violet flowers.

Blue—
the frequency
of light that lies
between violet and green.

Arthur Dove once said
Painting is music of the eyes.
A fleet of blues flute violet,
others oboe green.

Red seems closer to us than blue.

The more away an object,
the more it's drenched in blue—
observe each mood of mountains.

Blue eyes do not contain blue—
they just swallow less
blue light—
           it travels like bees
into the eyes of another.

In the Formal Wear Shop

His tie has fallen
from a paintbox:
a flock of parrots
flew and left
a kind of raucous cheek.

His plumage gleams
navy sleek,
his tape a mannered snake.

He is a bowerbird
collecting
satin jewels in rows,
each facet's edge
he dips to fold;
a tidy bowerbird.

He darts forward
and a little back,
he is guarding, showing,
pecks my eyes
and then he looks.

I'll propose to him (I think)
let's sail to Marrakesh,
unfurl the shirts,
cast into blue,
stain our souls
vermillion.

His eyes meet mine
(a borrowed blue)
he pecks and then he looks.
Slowly, I think again,
better to hem dreams up.

Intimidations

Each dawn has been a clotted pink;
                       the clouds, almost a red, infuse
unlikely ink into the sky. Camellias
climb in crimson confusion over fencelines,

And prunus plums arrange their frozen stars
as if auditioning them for small parts
                             in a Sisley or Corot.
My iceberg had the audacity to bloom pink,
                            and still I can sing away the spring.

In Lieu of a Statue

after *Housekeeping*
by Marilynne Robinson

The grass is blue with frost—
sharp as the small bones of feet.
The lilacs rattle: the stone steps
are too cold to sit upon.
I watch her in the honey-lit room
as she studies her face in the window.
I could throw a stone
but a window is not a lake:
it will not knit up again.
My grandmother used to say
close your eyes, remember how she was.
But the space against my lids
is flat and black as the sky.
If I could just *see* my mother—
it would not have to be her eyes,
it could be her lips or her throat.
How long since the moon-
lugged lake swallowed her?
Its water swims my bones.
The lilacs rattle like shrapnel.
If there had been snow
I could have made a statue.

Faith is Green

> *I'll settle for a sprig or two—*
> *The savour gracious, the leaves brimmingly green—*
> *as if never to say die.*

—Peter Steele, 'Rehearsal'

Where were you?
Not in the dark car
inside that shrunken space
on its slow glide to the boneyard.
Perhaps in the white lineage
of your brothers at the altar,
or traced on your crucifix—
your DNA, your trust.

Perhaps in the chapel glass,
the green shadow of tree,
the silhouette of wind—
the monkey that will not leave
its back: so many times,
in the pattern, your substance
of things: the wine, the wine,
the communion bread, forever
full and aloft as the moon.

After the silver cup,
the procession,
the soft blood of roses,
the car, the cold,
the stone steps, and your white brothers—
a force of herons or anxious angels,
pacing a spell
to portal you, or bring you back—
perhaps in the outdoor altar, its borders,
its fathom-green.

Not in the impossible grey of the sky
resistant as God's overcoat—
its flannel collar turned up.

Where are your sprigs of mint?
Behind the wall,
under the ground,
unseasoned
in the garden?
There is a tyranny of elm,
my footsteps,
and listening
for other audible patterns.

What Memory is Like

Officially, memory
is a cardboard box
sent to your home address.

Anyone who's received a memory
knows that it's untidy
as a fledgling's wing

crystalline as *crème brûlée*
and sometimes as acidic
as an ants' nest undone by rain.

And sometimes as welcome
as the neighbour's dog—
the one that meets you behind the fence
just as you reach your door.

Yet inside
is the ruby marble
you thought you'd lost
when you played for keeps.

Anyone who's received a memory
knows that you opened
a window into transparent wire.

Sometimes it will stain your hands.

Anyone who's received a memory
knows that its weight
is never more

than the insistent green
of an opened leaf.

Black on the Tongue

It was hot. I was ten. My towel knotted my waist, my wet bathers clung, chilled my skin with each gust of the wind. We were alone on an isthmus of land—wandered away, into shoulders of sand and odd squalls of berries. My yellow bucket grew patches of fruit; they were nuggets of sweet. I tasted salt on my fingers each time one nudged into my mouth. I can't recall what my uncle was wearing. I remember we laughed, that my towel slipped as I leant for more berries, that I ripped threads of pink when I tugged it from brambles that the wind was high, that I heard voices arriving like bells.

A Measure of Flying

The ironbark fringed the sky and scribbled our pool with leaves.
In summer we dived down, determined to rescue the blue.

I remember the tree, the rasp of bark on my legs, I tore soft
jewels from the trunk. They broke like unpicking a wound.

I'd shinny up a branch with a book or a balloon on a long leash
of string—play it out into blue, wait and then tug it back.

Sometimes I just sat on the rim, my legs hung in sheer edge,
eyes strung to that place where the sky melts into sun.

I had my own path to sky; a silver river on top of the sheds.
I ricocheted down the ripples, measured the fly of my feet.

Always that leap off the end, the sharp jar, the collapse
in deep grass, standing, earthed with an obstinacy—

knowledge that I'd really glimpsed flying. I grasped it
like wings and fell, unfeathered, again and again.

A Voice for Hands

The fine black hairs astonish me—
the clean neat fingernails.
I know I never will, but I want
to slide my finger along your wrist bone

to see if there really is an extra density
of being at the edge of you.

How else to explain why the world
falls in place behind you?
The first time I walked towards you
the footpath collapsed—

you moved towards me and receded
as though time had turned in on itself.

The plate-glass windows fledged
a pale galaxy: your skin, your face,
your eyes, quiet and distilled
as the points of stars.

I wish I could have measured you
with a compass and a star chart.

I have seen your hands since,
moulding the curve of a wine glass—
your fingertips pointed towards me.
I have watched your hands and the ring.

My hands have curled loosely as animals:
white, without hair, grammarless.

Lake Mungo

He wants to take her
where birds grew legs
long as rodeos,
and a re-imagined giant
wombat tends to disappoint.

He wants to drive her to a desert
where they ghosted her in ochre,
buried her, standing upright
by a milky singing lake.

He wants to walk with her
along a curve of shattered moon,
where human memory
unmade her long ago.

He wants to wake
where sand blows yesterday
from her face—
where there is nothing
but the terror of his faith.

How to Dive in Kelp Forest
kelp [ME *cülp(e)*, of unkn. origin]
—*The Concise Oxford Dictionary*

The stipes braid together, grow air-filled bulbs, float
   each frond towards the surface.
Do not jump into a mess of greenish-gold. Wait for the swing of the boat
  to move away. In thick kelp, the surface is not your friend;
   sometimes, even the bottom is not your friend.
Make a mental map:
   sketch it on your dive slate—plan your depth and time.
Canopies are so thick, it is like cave-diving
  —floating through an upper understorey of golden branches. Break stipes
  as if you are breaking a pencil—carry shears, but not a big Rambo knife. Don't start
      drowning
            and then discover your second stage is unfindable.
Did I mention the sculpins? The senoritas and Spanish shawls? The starfish,
   urchins and gorgonians?
      Don't penetrate so deep
        you don't know where out is. When surfacing, select a sand-patch
   where blue sky may be seen.

Apple Days

A poem should be palpable and mute
As a globed fruit ...
—Archibald MacLeish, 'Ars Poetica'

I smile each time
I see it from my window:
between the leaves
a twig of blossom, growing
out of season in the old apple tree;
a quirk of the weather
such unmeasured green,
a rain of leaves whispering
apple tree apple tree.
So dense.
So completely apple.
And all through these apple days
apples brood
large as infants' heads
welcome as teenage breasts
and leaves and leaves whispering
of apple tree.
So why not a tree more
full of being
than it has any right to be?

Sculpting into Mind
after Elizabeth Presa, sculptor

I love ephemeral things
lost discarded things
fluff human dust
flotsam the quietest things
can speak somewhere
a fold or ripple
a fault line in gauze
or skin I look for palest
grey in a flow of white
I look for wrinkles
in half-prints of sand
the quietest things can speak
I am a trail in dust I am
soft edge of my tracing

A Poem

is close
to a musical instrument.
It's a place
to leave your fingers
and your lips.
A poem aches to be
a woodland flute
but is more a piano.
Some poems are conch shells,
familiar as bone
in your hands. A poem
gleams in arc-light—
sparks from atolls in the dark.

... in the morning he found a small blue bowl on the porch outside his door. It looked to be full of rose petals, but he found when he picked it up that the rose petals were on top, the rest of the bowl—she must have swept them from the corners of her studio—was full of dead bees.
Robert Hass, 'A Story About the Body'

Almost Palimpsest

It was that time before dawn, and the words
were flapping again. They hung on black wings.
They gazed at him, waiting. He shut his eyes.
He glimpsed a swarm of shadows like a silence
before a hammering of bees. They massed now
a tumult of black, a writhing meniscus of wings.
They stormed him. He flung his arms out.
His body slowed to sculpture on the bed.

The Price of Honey

Her jewelled head lies low
in this gold-tessellated chamber.
Everywhere she looks, she sees
the sisterhood; there's no way out—
her wings have forgotten flight.
She pulses with eggs
at the heart of this strange
masonry of molten flowers.
One of her royal daughters wakes,
stings her sisters while they sleep;
shrill with treason,
the maiden bees mob
and butt their ancient queen
until her body explodes with heat.

Seeing the Pregnant Woman at Pompeii

You are there on the shelf
with the other artefacts: a series of urns
smooth as sculpted breasts, and beside you,
a shallow bowl, like a shell for a Venus rising.
But there is no Venus here, nor pearls.
Only a pity of coins
to hasten you to the truly dead.
You huddle with your knees up, hiding
what you cannot protect, your arms raised
to a face I cannot see. Abject, like the beggar
in a city street beside his bowl and the unnecessary sign:
please help me.
The pain of stone clings to you,
rags your edges, refuses comfort.

Discovered in 1977: *Petrogale persephone*

But I prefer Hades where I am more than just a pretty girl ...
—Ron Koertge, 'Persephone'

Her pelt is mauve-grey: uncombed as smoke.
The moment her young empty her milk pouch,
a foetus grips her fur. Her paths engrave the understorey—
she flirts with gardens. But pink flowers are a threat
and blindness infests the slipstreams of cats.
Once she dissolved into rainforest, invisible
(to science) until the year we discovered
how a bomb preserves urban habitat,
and a satellite transported a filigree of stars
to prove Miss Universe was black.

Flight

a feather cannot weigh why it has been abandoned
—Nathan Shepherdson, 'No. 27'

Feathers laid out:
brushes to paint sky
or swords left for a god
of weightlessness.

The gift-giver gone.
Feathers laid out:
as if a child began
to make a bird.

Feathers—
as if the bird
just slipped
its clothes off for a moment.

A militia of starlings
low-flying, and a cat—
petal-pawed, flowing.
Red on the pavement

and clumps on wires.
Doves, looking down—
like humans standing at a funeral.
But silent completely.

Bringing You Home

You've stained my sleep again
and your tiny clothes tangle their limbs
in my washing machine. So many headless bodies
and now your wriggly purple flesh,
two white straps on a new white nappy, wet,
wet, wet, urine soaks it, and you, and me,
before I can hook your spider legs
back into their flowered net.
Dark silk clings to your skinny neck,
yet no spider ever lifted sounds like this.
Your eyes are marbles in a slow slot-machine
and there, you've scratched your face again.
It's time to snare those starfish hands—
But God, how to blunt such silver flecks.

Instructions for Weaning a Baby

Tell her it's overrated.

Tell her she will learn to love the taste of salt—
salt on her tongue, grit of the ocean.

Tell her, in the morning the sea is milk.

Tell her about the sea-line—
where the sea and the sky seem to meet.

Tell her, in full summer, naked on a beach,
the sun drenching her skin is not unlike
a flood of milk.

Tell her many things
are warm and silky in spring.

Tell her to drink an armful of roses.

Tell her to slice a peach from its skin,
let it melt on her tongue,

find a way to that room—

amber-lit as a jar of peach jam
just cooling in a pantry.

A Mermaid's Story

Gender dysphoria is not a 'lifestyle choice'
—The Charing Cross Gender Identity Clinic

All my life I have been troubled
by her story.
Have I raised you inside it?
Every step hurts.
Like walking on glass.
Like knowing the window
is already broken.
At four years old they stitched
your eyes
because your lashes cut them.
At five you rubbed your tongue
until you could not speak.
You are learning
how to walk backwards.
One day there will be more
blood on the sheets:
may your voice
wake you.

Mycophobia

Humus
Found a mouth
Shaped its rotten music
A slippery blooming
Fluting and folding
At first I denied it
Just a ragged box
Well beyond recycle
Left to dissemble
Signage of can't be bothered me
But it's become viral
It's singing D
Decomposition
Like a casting of death
The host was there before
Its keys
Are in my brickwork
What else
Could I tell you?

Breast Imaging

I see the bird first,
her head snuggled down
into the green of herself.
Her tail is a handle.
A handle to hold a bird.
A handle to tether a breast.
This is a breast made of stone.

*

A pyramid
of apples, untouched,
and a woman,
calm and complete
as a dinner plate,
her face floats
just below the black glass.

*

I bivouac near the window
far away from the man.
Beside him
a frail statue,
her two small breasts.
I gift him the dark woman,
her two blind breasts.

*

Are you here for review?
There is always a talker.
My companion is clean-limbed
and bronze-skinned,
folds her vowels like a venetian blind,
her bones are strong
as handrails.

*

She navigates, close as a lover,
captures black bubbles,
maps echoes,
locates a white button
like a core in the dark.
She wipes clear gel
off my skin.

*

The orchids are rising
from the river of black glass.
I can feel the heartbeat
of the ceiling. The talker's beside me
in a wheelchair. The orderly
kindles the lift.
We descend.

Frames for Better or Worse

(i) *A marriage made in hospital*

It was like missing Italy
or standing in a bleached chimney—
this anaesthetic marriage.
He wanted duty to be swift and fresh
as a prayer: they kissed like an armistice.
Like a rainy town in winter.
Like two battalions at the front
who never believed absolutely
in career.

(ii) *Home*

You'll find no yellow spindles
in the corner of white paper, darling.
No blue lines to stand in for the sky.
No sprigs of green.
No pixie hat atop a pastel square.
No stick figures humming fingernail smiles.
I'm talking about a hurtle
smack bang into the white house itself,
darling; before there's time
to find the door.

(iii) *Nursery rime*

You dawned like winter sunlight
pale gold on the walls. A glitter
edging my shut window. Translucent
as if you swallowed a morning star.
Your breath unsettles like dust
of gardens. Your fingers take root
in air. You are a cloud growing
flowers, a bird-house with womb-
song in your eyes. You, origami child:
now sleep refolds your baby mask.

(iv) *A family of birds*

We dream on the wall that holds
us, in the shape that moulds us.
We cannot finish,
cannot dismantle the idea
of flight: too many birds
grace the window.
Our necks outstretch our wings—
our formation the lost art of arrows.
How might bodies turn into song?
Dust roosts in odd corners.

We Outgrow Love like Other Things

When I wake, the sun
scrims the tree and the sky
pours out its clear blue.
Glitter of morning.
I will bury you with champagne
and two glasses.

I will bury you
with a piece of cloth.
Your erstwhile clothes.
I can't remember the smell of you.

I will find my sage-green fleece,
cut out a scrap, draw up a chair
close to a bonfire,
let the woodsmoke enter.

I will take it down to the sea,
thread it on a small twig,
let the sea-wind ride it all day,
grains of sand will nest in it.
I will rub it against the trunk of a tree,
let it sleep in pine needles.

I will bury you with a piece of granite,
like the shards I collected as a child.
I loved the way the quartz
half-fell from the stone,
glittering like blind eyes,

in my hand
a compacted galaxy—
                        a dark
small enough to test against my skin.

In the Cemetery

You there—I—here—
With just the Door ajar
—Emily Dickinson, 'I cannot live with You'

Graves tread
oblong shadows
on the silvered path—
primitive dominoes

The boy statue
stubborn as bone—
his mind's gesture
disrupts a grey sky

The gravestone, clean
as a new kitchen,
red moths on the black—
hieroglyph roses

Near the rust-fingered wall
her white hair
and unstitched grin—
light as air, waiting

This World is not Conclusion
i.m. Miranda Ann Barnych, 1980–1997

New grass on the clifftop shoulders her smile
You drag your body down the hill

Wonder why a cairn of shattered silver
and plastic roses satisfies as prayer

You wonder why the jellyfish moon punishes
a solid blue sky

Why you heard chopsticks clatter on polished rice

You wonder if green counts time like an abacus

Why there is an aftertaste of white

Metamorphosis
i.m. Franz Kafka, 1883–1924

Cathedral-bird cawdaw jackerdaw,
dark-plumaged passerine bird,
a jackdaw is *kavka* in Czech.

Genus of crows and ravens,
it calls in a metallic *chyak chyak*.
Cathedral-bird cawdaw jackerdaw.

Jackdaws are harbingers of rain,
their underwings are wire grey,
and *kavka* means jackdaw in Czech.

His sisters Elli, Valli and Ottla
died in 'forty-one, two and three.
Cathedral-bird cawdaw jackerdaw.

Greeks tell that a jackdaw falls
seeking his kin in a dish of oil.
A jackdaw is *kavka* in Czech.

His beak and throat are clattering:
he calls in a metallic *chyak chyak*.
Cathedral-bird cawdaw jackerdaw.
A jackdaw is *kavka* in Czech.

The Hope Stone

They rise from the stone—
four letters, like thin galaxies
across its dark-knit dome.
As if a giant raked up the stars,

compacted them into gritty clay,
then coiled and strung out
hope
across a stolid sky.

The word contests the stone,
yet the letter *e*
is a face in profile,
screaming, and the *o* is opening

and the night seems small,
like an old boot
scuffed at the toe. As if
there could be another one.

The Striped Moth
(in the Melbourne Museum)

At 5 pm your wings will hang with shadow.
Now, they feed on light. Do you remember
tapping at the window, frantic as a tiny bell?
Or is your soul composed—a forest of shadows?

A tiger is latched in you: those eyes crouch
like stars and your pelt is stopped as a tinderbox.
A tree expands in the veins of your wings—
counts one night and half a dawn—signs off.

from Notes on Art and Dying

25.10.2008 *How to paint a rose*

A glass case displays the steps for painting a rose. It is like looking down through still water at a catalogue of the artist's mind. First, the watercolours on white paper: orange-red, orange-purple, purple-red ... like a row of summer's icy-poles melting. Second, words in neat rows of type on the page: *The rose grows in the walled gardens of Highgrove and is the most glowing of reds, oranges and purples—at times I had to blink to rest my eyes from its brilliance.* The finished Botanical lies beside the words. A single red rose, head composed high on its stem, elegant, vigorous, more luminous than its foil of white. Like the first and final drafts of a poem. The completed rose is perfect in every detail: emblematic, cultivated to sharp points of lineage, the petals soft as blood. The real rose lies beside its avatar. How do you draw a rose dying?

Film

after *Film*
by Tacita Dean

i
A toe winces in the corner
As if inside a shoe.
So many frames
Inside frames.
Is a panelled door
A building spliced into rooms?
I cling to possibility,
Two figures blur to three—
Glimpse of lakes on the moon.
Spots of red
Spark like jewels,
Disrupt my living.

ii
In this tunnel of light
No paintbox of blood:
White noise
Flickers polka-dots,
Around its navel
The waterfall runs backwards.
The single pine at dusk
Collects pink neon spots—
Like wormholes.
Like cracks that distil
What light there is.

iii
My personal Everest
Seen from above—
Sharp as a shredded moon.
White nitrogen
Pulses its lost horizon,
A chimney blows pompoms
into a no-comment sky.
The doorway clings to blue,
Mountains uluru the red.
Pale ocean sweeps in real time,
Sweeps it out again.

iv
Giant bubbles parry
Downward drift,
Stay intact,
Comply.
A black-and-white orange
Globes so close
It almost dreams a breast.
An egg sits on an apartment ledge.
The quality of flower-pink
Is a contract she clutches in one hand
Not like Mondrian's return
To infinite flower-shops
Nor pared-back Chagall.

v
A white-barred pigeon pecks
The edge of a field.
The escalator offers up,
But only travels down.
Black slate is spilt
In filmic light:
The floor's too deep,
The light too shallow.
Nothing lives
Outside its apparition.
Nothing not known at last.

Gouache, Sheep Skulls, Fence Bracket

after *Monaro*
by Steven Holland

I

Animals in Venetian masks
stare through floral constellations;
a strange surfacing
of herbal machinations
and cloven-hoof memories;
a fondness, somewhere
for droughtless green.

Look closer.
The skulls are singing,
more like bird-beaks than sheep.
Forget-me-nots break
across bone
as if souls commune,
call back,
jigsaw a collective self.

II

This is about a rasp of sheep;
a four-cornered star
shining the sacrament
of limited diagonals,
and yet, in sockets of dark,
a kind of backward birthing.

How to place gouache
and not annul the souls of sheep.
How to stamp passports
of those who dream the inner side
of crates—
a floating, rocking panic.

Their flowers are dispensed.
Ragged edges stumble
into blackened bone.
Quietly, they bleed
in palest pink.

For Cornflowers to Sing

Blue must be stolen.
There must be purple
plums, cherries, telling us
blue insists on the flower.

The silence of the jar
must be the centre
which grows the painting,

Unlatches stillness,
resists composition,
detonates the seasons.

For cornflowers to sing
each line must scar
its making.

There must be light
and the idea of a window.

In each fold of creamy linen,
blue corners
crouching under the table.

For cornflowers to sing
they must be fallen.
Blue slalom.
White grave of the table.

The Vase Imposes

The adoration of the flower for its own sake begins with the rise of 'Flower-Masters', towards the middle of the seventeenth century.
—Kakuzō Okakura, The Book of Tea

The Master of Flowers respects
the economy of nature—

his scissors and minute saw
contort muscles
and dislocate bones.

He diets flowers
with salt
and sometimes alum,

confines them
in slim vessels, quells
a mad thirst with still water.

He cannot pause
by a bamboo fence

to converse
with a wild chrysanthemum.

He must not salvage flowers
cut down by a storm.

He must not drift his boat
into multitudes of lotus.

White plum-blossom
is forbidden
when snow lies in the garden.

Does he wonder
if flowers are his risen sisters?

Southern Ice Porcelain

This whiteness assembles
only whiteness. These bowls
are so perfect they must exist
in an alphabet of shape.
Their stillness is an argument
for eternity. He mined dark
clay, drove out its titanium,
his hands and his wheel caught
form as it slid from shadow.
He stood them in a diamond
blaze of fire, inscribed wind's
flow in summer grass, a dying
wife's journal: his vessels wait
for the company of angels.

The Wabi-sabi Storage Jar

It's large enough to lair an animal.
Gravelled, rich-red, its slabs
Roughly rhyme around its opening.
One smooth black lip binds its craggy lip:
Night kisses a mountain.
It is pocked in silver as if
Fire dragged its starlight to the surface:
A crime of green
Found a home here
When flame collided with clay.

Everest

(i) *the blue inkwell of the sky*

As a boy I remember thinking how is it possible to climb into the sky
My father gave action to my dreams   he taught me to climb small mountains
I have a theory that people climb for the smell of it
I felt more like an astronaut   no clouds   a curving horizon
Just the flapping prayer flags   the beat and heave of my heart and my lungs
You cannot imagine how beautiful
    small tissue notelets   Ang Lakpa told me to throw them
into the air   they hung there   caught in the updraughts
about twenty feet above our heads

(ii) *its wings and drops and cliffs*

I was travelling in a whiteout   I fell head over heels
my ice-axe had no bite in the snow
I could not feel my feet because of frostbite
the torches were not working
night was falling and the wind was picking up
I just slumped into the snow and cried
tears for lost friends
Some of us lost all our toes and some fingertips
The summit is a narrow place
Twenty people were already there
I descended about twenty feet and sat alone

The Danger of Lilies

Their dark leaves are chiming
ascension ascension
and still they reach up:
wide open, they shimmer
citrus-greens infuse starry-pinks,
stamens so neat: thin capsules
pressed in relic-gold paint,
each satin throat clean as epiphany.
It's hard to believe they wrestled
up from underground.
Smug inverted parachutes,
they devour sky
distil each scrap of liminal—
disrupt the *other* of cats.

Two Voices

after 'La Voix'
by Charles Baudelaire

My cradle leant towards the library—
Latin ash and Greek dust mingled,
fiction pressed its kiss on science, gods
and fable. The space between my eyes
was blacker than my name, and sweet
as the yolk of daffodils, two voices spoke
to me: the earth is made of honeyed cake,
each bite will spike exquisite scent upon
your tongue. The other whispered: only
dreams eclipse the memory of your face,
and so my eyes are full of sky, and even
flint of sharpest wine cannot spark
my name—a cradle lies in this abyss
and the moon burns in my pocket.

Writing with the Left Hand

You've lost the hand that writes? Learn to write with the other hand.
—Hélène Cixous, 'Coming to Writing'

Moles channel under my skin—if they break the surface,
what then? A rash. A plague. Hands could atrophy waiting
for that mute continent, then a morbidity of doctors!
I could be bandaged as a mummy, inside a polished tree!
And what hands can understand inside such white, such
practised bindings? What rhythm invokes restriction? What
timbre its keynote? Yes, best to cut one off. Right is the left hand.
Now is the left hand and blood on the table. Red on white
holds no shadow. I will use the ink from my dead hand.

Notes

Part One

'Flute of Milk' is in conversation with John Banville's *The Sea* (Picador, 2005).

'In Lieu of a Statue' is in conversation with Marilynne Robinson's *Housekeeping* (Farrar, Straus and Giroux, 1980).

'What Memory is Like' is after 'What the Brain is Like' by Miroslav Holub, *Poems Before & After* (Bloodaxe Books, Second Expanded Edition, 2006) and Debbie Lim's unpublished poem, 'What the Brain is Like'.

'How to Dive in Kelp Forest' is adapted from the text 'Tip Sheet on How to Dive KELP in California' by Scott and Nancy Barnett (2005, p. 1–8).

Part Two

'Discovered in 1977: *Petrogale persephone*': in 1977 the endangered Proserpine Rock-wallaby (endemic to the Whitsundays) was discovered, the US president decided to test the neutron bomb, and the *Miss Universe* beauty contest was won by a black woman for the first time.

'We Outgrow Love like Other Things' is the first line of an untitled poem by Emily Dickinson.

'This World is not Conclusion' is the first line of an untitled poem by Emily Dickinson.

'Metamorphosis': 'Cathedral-bird cawdaw jackerdaw' are obsolete names for jackdaw.

'Film': '*Is a contract she clutches in one hand*' and '*paintbox of blood*' are from 'The Fall' by Jordie Albiston '*Nothing* not known at last' is a minor adaptation of 'Nothing not known at last.' from 'Everythings', a prose-poem by Alex Skovron from his paper 'The Elephant in the Clock: A Personal Fantasia', presented at the Carmelite Centre, August 28 2013.

'*from* Notes on Art and Dying/25.10.2008. *How to paint a rose*': the poem is a response to an exhibition by Anne O'Connor at the Mornington Pennisula Regional Gallery. The lines in italic are by Anne O'Connor, botanical artist.

'For Cornflowers to Sing' is a response to Brett Whiteley's *Still Life with Cornflowers*. The title is an adaptation of 'for the cornflowers/to sing ...' from 'Cornflowers' by Robert Adamson.

'The Vase Imposes' is in conversation with Chapter 6 of *The Book of Tea* by Kakuzō Okakura (Dover, 1964).

'Everest' was adapted from *Everest: Reflections From The Top*, edited by Christine Gee, Garry Weare and Margaret Gee (Rider, 2003).

www.ingramcontent.com/pod-product-compliance
Lightning Source LLC
Chambersburg PA
CBHW020341170426
43200CB00006B/452